LEADING WOMEN

Indira Gandhi

SARA SCHUPACK

Cavendish
Square

New York

Published in 2014 by Cavendish Square Publishing, LLC
303 Park Avenue South, Suite 1247, New York, NY 10010

First Edition

Website: cavendishsq.com

This publication represents the opinions and views of the author based on his or her personal experience, knowledge, and research. The information in this book serves as a general guide only. The author and publisher have used their best efforts in preparing this book and disclaim liability rising directly or indirectly from the use and application of this book.

CPSIA Compliance Information: Batch #WS13CSQ

All websites were available and accurate when this book was sent to press.

Library of Congress Cataloging-in-Publication Data
Schupack, Sara.
Indira Gandhi / Sara Schupack.
p. cm. — (Leading women)
Includes bibliographical references and index.
Summary: "Presents the biography of Indira Gandhi against the backdrop of her political, historical, and cultural environment"—Provided by publisher.
ISBN 978-0-7614-4955-3 (hardcover) ISBN 978-1-62712-113-2 (paperback)
ISBN 978-1-60870-712-6 (ebook)
1. Gandhi, Indira, 1917-1984—Juvenile literature. 2. Prime ministers—India—Biography—Juvenile literature. 3. Women prime ministers—India—Biography—Juvenile literature. 4. India—Politics and government—20th century—Juvenile literature. I. Title. II. Series.
DS481.G23S34 2012
954.04'5092—dc22 [B]
2011009224

Editor: Deborah Grahame-Smith   Art Director: Anahid Hamparian   Series Designer: Nancy Sabato
Photo research by Connie Gardner

Printed in the United States of America

CONTENTS

CHAPTER ONE

Complex Influences

I NDIRA GANDHI WAS A POWERFUL WOMAN leader of a new, diverse nation. In her time India was new as a country, though the culture and history were ancient. Indira brought a complex combination of heritage and traditions to the job of prime minister. She was Indian, she was a woman, and she was a member of the Nehru family, whose members grew up watching the independence movement develop—and, finally, after much struggle, succeed. Indira once said,

> **India has not ever been an easy country to understand. Perhaps it is too deep, contradictory and diverse, and few people in the contemporary world have the time or inclination to look beyond the obvious, especially because in our country we have the greatest scope of free expression of opinion and all differences are constantly being debated.**

Mohandas Gandhi, or Mahatma Gandhi—not related to Indira—was a close family friend. His independence movement, which set the tone for years to come, was based in the country's masses. For Gandhi, the village was an important center for the voice and identity of the nation. He also firmly opposed materialism. While Indira and her father did not follow Mahatma Gandhi's philosophy to the letter, Mahatma greatly influenced them.

Father and daughter: Jawaharlal Nehru and Indira, 1964

No matter whose philosophy prevailed, village life was—and still is—central to India's history and politics. Today, 750 million of the nation's 1.1 billion people inhabit rural settings, and half of India's villages do not have paved roads. More than half the nation's women have not learned to read or write.

Indira Gandhi's legacy included efforts to reach and serve a huge and diverse population. The country she was to lead had a personality as layered and deep as her own. Edward Luce comments that, "Societies are in some ways like human beings. Things that have happened to them in their formative years have a tendency to shape their decision and character long after those events have lost their context." All of these elements shaped both India and the woman who was to lead it.

CONFLICTS AND CONTRADICTIONS

Indira also inherited a lot of disagreement. Indira's father, Jawaharlal Nehru, Mahatma Gandhi, and Bhimrao Ambedkar, who is less known outside of India but considered a very important figure in that country's history, all had differing views on village life and science and technology. Gandhi found science suspiciously connected to Western values and influence, while Ambedkar saw no such difficulty and advocated scientific advancement. Ambedkar, the first Indian statesman of the "untouchable" caste (the lowest social class), who struggled up from rural poverty, had no romantic views of the village as did the more privileged Gandhi and Nehru. Ambedkar assumed the position of India's first law minister and contributed to India's 1950 constitution; he fought to grant all adults the right to vote. In spite of his huge contributions, the Indian caste system still affects politics today. All of these unresolved issues were part of Indira's India.

Indira was an independent thinker who strived with passion and determination to do what was best for her country, regardless of whose ideas or platforms impacted her decisions. Nonetheless, she was a product of her time, her family dynamics, and her personal development. Nehru was not only her father, whom she adored and admired, but also India's longest-serving leader before Indira took charge, so he had great influence on both his daughter and his nation. Within his long term as prime minister (1947-1964), Nehru experienced tensions and contradictions due to the conflicts mentioned above, as well as other sources. He represented democracy and modernity, yet the Nehrus were a dynastic family. For many generations, power remained in their hands: Motilal, Indira's grandfather; Jawaharlal Nehru, Indira's father; Indira herself; Indira's son, Rajiv Gandhi; and Rajiv's wife, Sonia Gandhi.

The conflict between breaking with Britain and maintaining elements of British culture impacted both politics and home life in India. In a way, to be modern was to be Western, yet India was struggling to break free from Britain. To be independent meant to be democratic, yet it seemed one family held the monopoly on power. Luce tells us, "On the many occasions when Nehru was arrested by the British and imprisoned, he would, as a rule, eat cornflakes, fried eggs, bacon, and fried tomatoes, before submitting to his captors. Gandhi would have a drop of lime juice and some goat's milk."

Differing views on how big and powerful India's government should be affected Nehru's leadership. These disagreements linger to this day. One view is that the state should have vast power and reach, so that leaders can fix problems and keep a very diverse nation unified. At the same time, Indians have always been ambivalent about making money and doing business. Wealth and commerce are good for the country, yet some Indians view material

THE BRITISH RAJ

The motives behind imperialism are complex. England's interest in India was both economic and political. Britain's rule over India, which lasted from 1858 to 1947, is referred to as the British Raj (*raj* means "reign" in Hindustani). Business and politics merged when the British East India Company came under the rule of Queen Victoria. As England annexed new territories, it reaped the benefits of commodities such as spices, cotton, and opium. Indians participated and profited as well, particularly in the role of emissaries who connected rural and urban centers. Stability was another motive for England, because of the Napoleonic Wars (1799–1815) and Russian expansion toward Afghanistan in the 1830s. Britain's presence in India served to balance the power.

With imperialism comes racism. To justify taking territories by force and installing home leadership, colonial leaders sometimes convince themselves that native people are backwards and need to be "civilized." The British took exactly this stance. There was widespread disrespect and disregard for Indian history and customs.

Through development projects such as railroads, telegraph networks, and uniform postal services, the British set themselves up as a permanent force bringing improvements to India.

In the late nineteenth century, there were beginnings of self-rule, through elections of local representatives to legislative councils. Still, not everyone could vote. Only a small group of upper-class Indians qualified.

World War I changed India's standing in the world. Indian soldiers fought side by side with the British. Under its own name, India became one of the founding members of the League of Nations in 1920.

More and more Indians earned the right to vote. Still, the low literacy rate made it difficult for people to exercise this right. In 1935, the Government of India Act authorized independent legislative assemblies in all of British India's provinces, to be united under a central government. World War II complicated the situation, however, because of the viceroy, Lord Linlithgow. He was the British official set up in India who answered to England. He declared war on India's behalf without consulting the local Indian leaders. This is part of what motivated the Quit India movement, led by Mohandas Gandhi.

The religious divisions that would always plague India caused much strife during this time as well. Independence did come, but only after much violence and geographic division. Muslim areas entered a new nation, Pakistan, and the provinces of Punjab and Bengal were partitioned along religious lines. It was the mainly Hindu and Sikh areas that became the new India.

Two greats sharing a joke: Nehru (*left*) and Mohandas Gandhi (*right*) at the All-India Congress committee meeting, 1946

prosperity as impure. The spiritual and the pragmatic often go hand in hand in India.

For Nehru, however, spiritualism was quite general. Impatient with the self-sacrificing, determined spiritualism of Mahatma Gandhi, he made secularism part of his platform and policies. Nehru did not think that all religions were bad. Instead, he felt that religion and politics should remain separate, aside from the government's responsibility to ensure freedom of religion. For example, Nehru insisted

INDIA'S CASTE SYSTEM

India's caste system is complex and controversial. While it originated in Hinduism, where there were four communities or groups arranged in a hierarchy, most powerful to least, a social system developed from it with more castes, or levels. The word itself in its original language, closer to "jat," meant a community with language and culture in common. Europeans in India changed the word to what is used today, "caste." Before Indian independence, the British made lists of castes as part of their effort to rule India. Government lists include these categories: Scheduled Castes, Scheduled Tribes, and Other Backward Classes. As odd as those titles sound, later, India used some of the same lists in deciding which disadvantaged groups or castes were deserving of extra support, similar to affirmative action.

Large groups, castes, or jats are divided into smaller ones, sometimes based on occupation or beliefs. The hierarchy gets muddled within the subgroups, for example, certain jobs have different status in different parts of India. The traditional castes by occupation are the Brahmins at the top, who are associated with peace, wisdom, and faith. Kshatriayas are leaders, expected to be resourceful, heroic, and generous. Next come Vaishya, who do the work of trade and agriculture, and finally at the bottom, Shudras. They are meant to do the work of service, menial labor, and were the "untouchables." Usually people are expected to marry within their caste. Originally, a person was born into a caste and could not move "up," and had no choice of job. That has changed today. Even though the caste system is not legal any more, social divisions and ideas about rigid social classes do persist. The castes are starting to loosen up, though, especially in the cities.

that Muslims be given equal rights; this deeply angered Hindu revivalists from the Bharatiya Janata Party (BJP). Thus, Indira inherited a thorny religious conflict as well.

The Nehru-Gandhi dynasty, in which Indira held a prominent place, impacted India in huge ways. The family introduced three main trends: democracy, secularism, and socialism.

DEMOCRACY IS NEITHER EASY NOR OBVIOUS

Democracy in India is complex. India is an unusual country in part because it achieved full democracy before it had a large middle class, and before its literacy rate topped 50 percent. That every citizen could and should have a voice—regardless of conflicts, differences, and difficulties—says something about the determination of India's leaders to change their nation quickly, especially since other developing nations were not embracing democracy at the time. As part of India's strategy for rapid change, each party had a visual symbol, so that people who were illiterate could vote without having to read or write a candidate's name. For example, the Congress Party's image was a hand; the BJP, a lotus flower; and the Samajwadi Party, a bicycle. It was a brave democracy, but a harsh one too, with twenty-four party coalitions and all sorts of conflicts and power struggles. Even within a democracy, upper castes and elites have long tended to dominate Indian politics. This, too, was Indira's inheritance.

Conflicts and contradictions demonstrate what is so fascinating about India. Luce explains that "India is finally emerging as an important economic and political force on the world stage while remaining an intensely religious, spiritual, and, in some ways, superstitious society is unusual by the standards of many countries."

HOW DO WE READ HER?

Understanding who Indira was as a person and a leader is not easy: her gender, the history of her family and country, and her personal quirks and gifts all add to the story. When we look at someone or something that is foreign and far away, we sometimes think of it as exotic and, therefore, strange and impossible to understand. The exoticism that people in the West may see in Eastern cultures can warp their assessments of people and cultures from those regions. Edward Luce suggests that "although the West has also produced many balanced and scholarly assessments of India over the past 250 years, the views of most ordinary Westerners have been tinged with either the dismissive or the romantic (as many still are)." To complicate matters further, Indians themselves sometimes promote a romanticized version of their culture.

One may also view women as somehow not the norm, often without even realizing it. This additional kind of exoticism might also warp one's view. In other words, if Indira behaved in a strong, decisive, or bullying way, do we say she is behaving like a man? That might not be fair. Similarly, should we expect her to be a sensitive, gentle, and maternal leader because she is a woman? This, too, is unfair. And how often do we consider gender in male world leaders? While this biography of Indira Gandhi does address the fact that she is female, she viewed herself as a leader, not as a woman leader. In Indira's own words,

> I am not a feminist and I do not believe that anybody should get a preferential treatment merely because she happens to be a woman. . . . I do not regard myself as a woman. I am a person with a job.

CHAPTER TWO

Her Beginnings

J AWAHARLAL NEHRU, INDIRA GANDHI'S father, had a British-style upbringing. He was at one point very wealthy. Nehru had an Irish tutor and went to England for high school and college. He grew up in a household with one hundred servants. His mother, Swarup Rani, however, was a very traditional and devout Hindu. She wore saris, bathed in the Ganges River, was a vegetarian, and understood but did not speak English. The women in Nehru's childhood home spoke Hindi, although his father, Motilal, required that the family speak English at the dinner table. Motilal was actually expelled from his caste for refusing to undergo a purification ceremony when he came back from England. In the Nehru household, women, along with their associated beliefs and languages, had less power than men. Thus, Nehru's childhood was one of cultural clash, spiritual confusion, and gender division. These contradictions shaped Nehru and his later parenting of Indira.

Motilal chose Jawaharlal's education and career for him. He selected law in England. Jawaharlal was not so enthusiastic about his studies, and instead he overspent his allowance and had a lot of fun in England. His father even chose Jawaharlal's bride, Kamala Kaul, when she was only twelve years old. Following Western views of romantic love, Jawaharlal resisted this last command. He did end up marrying Kamala, but not until she was older. At age sixteen, she was sent to Allahabad to be "trained" to be his wife—her education included instruction in

Jawaharlal Nehru as a boy (seated) with his mother, Swarup Rani Nehru, and father, Pandit Motilal Nehru. Circa 1899

European manners and habits. This strict and authoritarian parenting style was not unusual for the time, nor was it unusual to think of European manners as representing refinement and success. In some ways, Jawaharlal reacted against his upbringing as a young man and later as a parent, but he could never entirely free himself from his background.

HERE COMES INDIRA

On the stormy night of November 19, 1917, Indira Nehru was born. She was small, only 4 pounds, with a delicate mouth and features. Her lovely big eyes and full head of hair stood out, as did her relatively large nose (a feature that never pleased her).

In many Asian cultures, boys are preferred. This was the case in Indira's family as well, although the quiet, unstated disappointment in her gender was not dramatic. She later commented,

> While my family was not orthodox enough to consider the birth of a girl child a misfortune, it did regard the male child a privilege and a necessity.

To Jawaharlal Nehru, what was more significant than his baby's gender was that her birth coincided with the Russian Revolution. History and politics were always in the forefront of his mind.

A SERIOUS CHILDHOOD

In a way, Indira was not treated as a girl, nor was she treated as a child. A busy, politicized household had no time for child's play.

One of her first memories was at age three, when the family built a bonfire to burn all English cloth as part of a boycott for the independence movement. Suddenly the comfortable admiration of England and English products was over. Little Indira was asked to burn her doll, also a British product, but to her the doll was a companion. This was very painful. She obliged, but she got sick immediately afterward.

By the age of five, Indira was working on her own *charkha* (spinning wheel), a symbol of the homespun cloth movement, which was

Little Indira with her parents, circa 1918

a widespread protest of British imports and British power. Her mother dressed her in a boy's khaddar (homespun cotton cloth) Congress Party volunteer uniform (the Congress Party represented the independence movement) and a Gandhi cap. People often mistook her for a boy. Later, when she exchanged letters with her father during his stints in prison, she often referred to herself as "Indu-boy." When describing her grandfather, Indira said he was both man and woman, with strength, intellect, and emotions, and she commented that she was much like him.

While Indira was young, her grandfather, Motilal, was still the family's leading patriarch. It was he who chose her name, which was a modernized version of his mother's name, Indrani. As his daughter's middle name, Jawaharlal chose the Buddhist name Priyadarshini, which means "dear to the sight" and "one who reveals the good." From the start, then, Indira faced powerful male expectations and a tender sense of duty and spirituality.

The other strong male influence on this little girl, besides her father and her grandfather, was Gandhi. Indira's mother, Kamala, accepted Mahatma Gandhi into the family, while the other women were more cautious. According to Katherine Frank, Swarup Rani, Indira's grandmother, "could not comprehend how and why this little man in a dhoti with his dietary and health fads should intrude on her family and advise them on both personal and political matters." To Indira, he was another elder in her home, and she sought advice from him. From Indira and all who were close to him, Gandhi earned the fond nickname Bapu.

THE WOMEN IN HER LIFE

In addition to the strong-willed, principled men in Indira's childhood, there were sharp tensions among the women. Indira's great-aunt, Bibi Amma, had been widowed at the age of eighteen. According to tradition, she gave up all material goods when her husband died. She never remarried, as it would have been considered disrespectful. Bibi Amma lived in Anand Bhawan (the "House of Joy") with the rest of the Nehru crowd. She was often judgmental, harsh, and unkind toward others, including Kamala and Swarup Rani. She was jealous of Kamala. Bibi Amma and Swarup Rani often left Kamala out, and they mocked and criticized her. One source of criticism was Kamala's limited English.

Despite her language gap and general shyness, however, Kamala spoke in public and participated actively in the independence movement. Kamala was often sick throughout her life. Physical illness and emotional stress coincided for her. Growing up, Indira helplessly watched as her mother suffered harsh treatment. She once commented about Kamala, "I saw her being hurt, and I was determined not to be hurt." Indira later stated that the press often overlooked her mother as an important influence on her; Kamala was simply left out of biographies and interviews. Indira said,

> As for any other child I suppose, my mother played a very special role. Among all these people, she too had a very strong character. But in a quiet way. And somehow she made a very deep impression. One tends to resist the influence of obviously strong people, and not be so concerned about that of people around them. Yet, if she believed in something, nothing could move her from it.

NOT AN ORDINARY EDUCATION

Although the people of India were becoming increasingly angry at England, and though they asserted themselves against colonial dominance, British culture was still a mark of power and respect. Even within the fight for independence, there were nuances and

MOHANDAS GANDHI

Mohandas Karamchand Gandhi was born in 1869 in a small town on the western coast of India. He came from a middle-class family, but his grandfather had earned prestige as prime minister of their town, Porbandar, and Mohandas's father had followed suit. Mohandas was very shy and was not a strong student. He was married at the age of thirteen. In spite of struggles in school, he was encouraged to follow in his father's footsteps, and so Gandhi went off to England to study law. His caste saw this act as a betrayal and excommunicated him for going abroad.

After briefly trying too hard to fit in by mimicking British fashions and ways, Gandhi learned that to become a true gentleman, he had to build his character from within.

Upon returning to India with a new law degree, Gandhi tried unsuccessfully to start up his business. He then accepted an offer to represent a firm in South Africa. Here, amid the cruelty of racism, Gandhi experienced a spiritual awakening, and his activism bloomed. He organized South Africa's Indian community to fight unfair legislation. It was also at this time that Gandhi developed his philosophy of nonviolent protest and peaceful, humble living. He brought his new confidence and wisdom back to India and applied them to the independence movement there.

Very quickly, Gandhi earned huge support. His methods of peaceful resistance empowered thousands and set an example for many others, including Martin Luther King Jr., who fought for civil rights in the United States. Gandhi never used violence, and he treated his enemies with respect and compassion.

This strategy brought attention to their bullying, hateful ways and thus earned him more support. Through the practice of *satyagraha*, which included strikes, fasts, and symbolic movements of peaceful protest, Gandhi and his followers challenged unjust British laws. Soon it became clear that independence from England was the only way to go. In 1947, India achieved its goal. Gandhi did not live to see India independent for long, however. He was assassinated on January 30, 1948.

Here are a few of Gandhi's many wise sayings:

"Freedom is not worth having if it does not include the freedom to make mistakes."

"Happiness is when what you think, what you say, and what you do are in harmony."

"When I despair, I remember that all through history the ways of truth and love have always won. There have been tyrants, and murderers, and for a time they can seem invincible, but in the end they always fall."

Indira at the bedside of the beloved Mohatma Gandhi, 1924

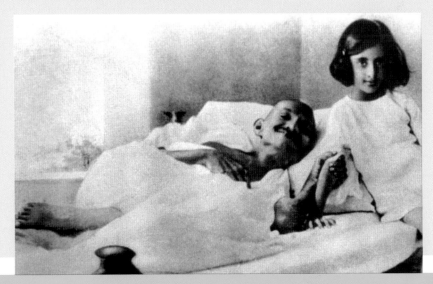

disagreements. Jawaharlal Nehru, Motilal Nehru, and Mohandas Gandhi had different visions. Jawaharlal wanted complete independence from England, while Motilal held on to his British tastes and possessions. This kind of ambivalence, even within a family, is not uncommon in colonial and postcolonial nations. The people of a colonized country want the bullies and oppressors to go away, and they want to define themselves as an independent nation. Yet it is not easy to shake the mind-set that power and status go together, and the culture that was in power for such a long time remains desirable because it symbolizes success.

Indira's education reflected these conflicting influences. It was Indira's mother, Kamala, who pushed for her education, and Motilal who paid for it. No one questioned that a British education was the best. Motilal did not seem particularly concerned with Indira's achievements, and he often encouraged her to miss school for long vacations. Was this partly because she was a girl? Perhaps. But because the Nehru family was passionate about politics, when Indira was not in school, she was still receiving an education. She spent much of her life abroad, studying in England and traveling throughout Europe. By the age of ten, when she returned to India, she was already a mature, independent person who spoke French, German, English, and Hindi.

Indira never quite felt comfortable in school, partly because what she learned there seemed so separate from what she experienced outside of school. She also struggled because most of her classmates were so different from her. Often she would dress in the British style even though her family was demonstrating loyalty to the homespun (homemade cloth) movement. While she was never keen on school, she was always fond of learning and reading. Early on, she loved reading about Joan of Arc, Giuseppe Garibaldi in Italy, and Simón Bolívar in South America, and one of her favorites was *Les Miserables*. These were all stories about heroism, standing up for the little guy, and the devastating effects of poverty and injustice.

At one point Indira studied with the renowned poet Rabindranath Tagore (also called Gurudev), who believed in independence through education. At Tagore's school, Indira explored art and music, and she found these forms of expression very moving. Here she describes Tagore's combination of nationalism and universalism:

> My father expressed the same idea in a different way when he declared that no one could be truly international unless he also was intensely national. . . . Gurudev Tagore was certainly a great poet. But he was also something bigger. Poetry was only one part of him. He was a very great human being and it was our great privilege to have him as a fellow Indian. It would not be right for us to claim that he belonged to India only.

Tagore's play *Chitrangada* intrigued Indira. The play's story focuses on the emancipation of women. The main character is a woman who disguises herself as a man, commands an army, falls in love, and then is granted a gift from a sage, of womanly graces. When she attracts the man she loves, she tells him her story and asks that he accept her for who she is.

While politics was never separate from the Nehrus' home life, work did take Jawaharlal away from his family. He got busier and busier, especially after 1936, when, based on Gandhi's suggestion and with Motilal's blessings, he succeeded his father as Congress Party president. One if his first acts of office was to issue a resolution for complete independence from Britain. Indira was with her father when he wrote it, and he asked her to read it aloud. It passed in the

A LETTER FROM PRISON

The following excerpt comes from a letter from Jawaharlal Neh-ru to Indira. The letter was eventually published in his book *Glimpses of World History*.

On your birthday you have been in the habit of receiving presents and good wishes. Good wishes you will still have in full measure, but what present can I send you from Naini Prison? My presents cannot be very material or solid. They can only be of the air and of the mind and spirit such as a good fairy might have bestowed on you—things that even the high walls of prison can-not stop. . . .

I must not therefore sermonize. But what am I to do, then? A letter can hardly take the place of a talk; at best it is a one-sided affair. . . . Imagine that I have made a suggestion to you for you to think over, as if we really were having a talk.

In history we read of great periods in the life of nations, of great men and women and great deeds performed, and sometimes in our dreams and reveries we imagine ourselves back in those times and doing brave deeds like the heroes and heroines of old. . . . But a time comes when a whole people become full of faith for a great cause, and then even simple, ordinary men and women become heroes, and history becomes stirring and epoch-making. . . . The year you were born in—1917—was one of the memorable years of history when a great leader, with a heart full of love and sympathy for the poor and suffering, made his people write a noble and never-to-be-forgotten chapter of history. In the very month in which you were born, Lenin started a great Revolution which has changed the face of Russia and Siberia.

And to-day in India another great leader, also full of love for all who suffer and passionately eager to help them, has inspired our people to great endeavor and noble sacrifice. . . . It is no easy matter to decide what is right and what is not. One little test I shall ask you to apply whenever you are in doubt. It may help you. Never do anything in secret or anything that you would wish to hide.

You are fortunate, I have said, in being a witness to this great struggle for freedom that is going on in our country. You are also very fortunate in having a very brave and wonderful little woman for your Mummie, and if you are ever in doubt or in trouble you cannot have a better friend. Good-bye, little one, and may you grow up into a brave soldier in India's service.

legislature, and Jawaharlal became a hero. From that day on, Anand Bhawan was not a private home any longer.

Indira spent a lot of her childhood alone and lonely. At one point, both of her parents were in prison. Her family, while prestigious, was now poor. Jawaharlal stopped earning money, and the family sold its family jewels. The tensions only continued, as Kamala fell terribly ill, Indira's father visited only briefly, and, for a time, Indira ignored Jawaharlal's letters.

A DYNAMIC LEADER AT AN EARLY AGE

Indira had always been invited into her father's political life; for example, she sat in on political meetings from an early age. In 1930, however, women all over the country were beginning to become more actively involved in civil disobedience. This began with the Salt March, a brilliant symbolic protest orchestrated by Gandhi. Even Kamala, who struggled with illness all her life, poured herself into the movement. It was she, along with a friend, who came up with the idea of the Vanar Sena, or "Monkey Brigade" (from the tale of Ramayan), a political group for children. Kamala put Indira in charge of a Vanar Sena group that soon bloomed to a size of almost one thousand kids! (In later years, Indira explained her founding of this group. She said that since the Congress Party would not accept her as a member because she was a minor, she wanted her own activist group).

At first Vanar Sena's members merely ran errands and carried messages, but soon they were also acting as spies, playing inno-cent children's games while eavesdropping on the police as they discussed arrests. Indira became famous for her leadership and work in this effort. She was known for her boy volunteer uniform and hat.

After her grandfather's death, Indira toured India with her father. This experience was eye-opening for many reasons, one of which was her first awareness of her nation's caste system. She says,

> At home, I had never been aware of caste, or anything like that, because there was no occasion to feel that someone was an untouchable. We had had untouchable servants from the very beginning. For instance, my grandfather's own servant, Hari, was an untouchable and he was like one of the family; he sometimes ate with us. But in the South, it was much stricter than in the North, and for the first time, the injustice of it came to me: there were whole streets where untouchables could not walk, which were reserved to 'Brahmins only.'

Because Indira took on so many adult worries and responsibilities as a child, her transition to adulthood was barely noticeable. She did start to make more of her own decisions, however—and soon she had some very big ones to make.

CHAPTER THREE

A Full Political Life

P UPUL JAYAKAR DESCRIBES INDIRA'S
strong, fiery, and inquisitive nature:

Indira was made of many elements. Her close association with the freedom struggle and the stalwarts of the independence movement had molded her life. In many ways she was a reflection of her father's mind. But her years in England and her association with Feroze Gandhi's left-wing friends, journalists and political thinkers had given her a radical conditioning. She was a rebel, antitraditional and antiestablishment, but a natural cautiousness kept her far away from any major Left commitments. Her early upbringing and her father's interests gave her a love of adventure, a fearlessness, and inbuilt sense of the secular; it also awakened a live curiosity and a constant search for new frontiers. From childhood she had an intimate feeling for nature. But in spite of her early exposure to intellectuals and powerful activists, she had lived within the confines of a society which hemmed her in, gave her little opportunity to reach out, meet people, explore the arts or investigate a life of the mind.

Indira's future husband, Feroze Gandhi (no relation to Mahatma Gandhi), had entered the scene long ago, first assisting Indira's mother in her efforts in the independence movement when Indira was a little girl, and then later, as Indira's suitor. Putting Feroze off at first, Kamala told him that Indira was too young; putting him off further, Indira said that the freedom struggle was more important than their courting. It was not a likely match,

Mohandas Gandhi, the Mahatma, with young Indira Nehru

as Feroze came from a different caste and religious affiliation. He had no birth certificate and was raised by an aunt, so his parentage was unclear. Feroze came from a family of Parsis, who traditionally supported the British, and they were very unhappy with his involvement with the Nehrus and the independence movement. He was frank, boisterous, and a big fan of food, drink, and flirting. Love was in the air, but as with so many other aspects of Indira's life, it was not simple.

After one stint abroad, Indira returned home to find a very distracted father. Jawaharlal had fallen in love with another woman, Padmaja Naidu, and they had a long relationship. He never divorced Kamala. One reason he offered was that he did not what to hurt his Indu, Indira. It is unclear how her father's affair affected Indira's feelings about him—or her general view of men—but her fiercely independent spirit and sympathy for her mother could only have been pushed further by this. Not long afterward, in Paris in 1937, Indira consented to marry Feroze, but she did not yet tell her father.

At this time, Indira was studying at Oxford. She was shy and felt out of place, but jovial Feroze drew her out. Oxford was a highly politicized place during the time leading up to World War II; its student union was sympathetic to left-wing philosophies, including communism. Indira also joined a radical Indian independence group. She was pressured into her first public speaking experience on behalf of the student group. On a stage, in front of crowds, she was so quiet that the audience could barely hear her, and people heckled her.

Indira's troubles were never just personal. The world was in upheaval, and her father took that to heart. Together, Indira and Jawaharlal toured India and felt the world's troubles as they hit home, including the exodus from Czechoslovakia of people fleeing Hitler. When Britain declared war against Germany, India was included as part of the Allied forces. Jawaharlal Nehru and his cohorts were torn; they strongly opposed fascism but still wanted to assert independence from Britain. The British, however, were not interested in worrying about India or tolerating dissent in this tumultuous hour. With Mahatma Gandhi's guidance, India settled on a symbolic protest of Britain's bullying assumption that India had no say in the matter, yet also offered general support for the war effort. This protest landed Nehru in jail yet again.

FAMILY AND POLITICS: AN IMPOSSIBLE BALANCE

Indira's mother, Kamala, faced her final illness in 1936. As usual, the whole family was torn between political duties and family bonds. Indira visited her mother frequently. Jawaharlal managed to see Kamala on February 8, their twentieth wedding anniversary, but he didn't stay long, as he had just been elected president of the Congress Party. He considered refusing the position in order to be with Kamala, but she urged him to go. Kamala started to withdraw. Nehru canceled his flight, but then Kamala's fever spiked and she started hallucinating. On February 28, she died.

While Nehru hoped that his daughter would become more involved in politics, she craved a "normal" life, with kids, a stable home, and music. Indira told him of her plans to marry Feroze. The preparations for her wedding were taking place as Japan attacked Pearl Harbor and took Singapore, Malaysia, and Burma. Colombo, Sri Lanka, was bombed. This was just too close to India. The Congress Party was trying to push England to grant India its independence. Gandhi was trying to talk Indira out of the wedding, which not only her family but also much of the public opposed, because she was Hindu and Feroze was Parsi. Indira persisted, however, and she and Feroze were married on March 16, 1942. She wore a pale pink sari made of yarn spun by her father while in jail, as part of the homespun movement.

Indira and Feroze Gandhi at their wedding, October 8, 1942

Indira's second public speaking experience happened after her honeymoon, when the Quit India movement was going strong and both her father and Mahatma Gandhi had been arrested. There were massive strikes and civil disobedience. Indira, who secretly distributed pamphlets and funds to further the cause, received a message that she was to be arrested. With gun-toting police closing in, and her new husband Feroze watching from a nearby hiding place, Indira bravely began to speak. One policeman put his hand on her arm, and that set off the crowd. Chaos followed. The police injured people with the butts of their guns, Feroze rushed forward to help his wife, and both Indira and Feroze were arrested. Says Indira,

The ride to the jail was a rather extraordinary one, for the police in my van were apparently so moved by my talking to them that they apologized, put their turbans at my feet, and wept their sorrow because of what their job compelled them to do!

This experience demonstrates not only the complexity of Indian politics at the time, but also Indira's sensitivity to all participants, even the "bad guys." She never saw things in black and white.

After eight months in prison, Indira was released due to poor health. The time in prison had changed her. She felt more united with her father and the independence movement than ever before: "What a world of difference there is between hearing and seeing from the outside and the actual experience. No one who has not been in prison for any length of time can ever visualize the numbness of spirit that can creep over one when, as Oscar Wilde writes: 'Each day is like a year, a year whose days are long.' . . . debarred not only from outside company or news but from all beauty and colour, softness and grace. . . . All things pass and so did this. My unexpected release was like coming suddenly out of a dark passage—I was dazzled with the rush of life, the many hues and textures, the scale of sounds and the range of ideas. Just to touch and listen was a disturbing experience and it took a while to get adjusted to normal living."

MOTHERHOOD

On August 20, 1944, Indira gave birth to her first son, Rajiv. She never got to spend much time with her children, yet she felt motherhood was one of her most important roles. Later, she commented, "To a woman, motherhood is the highest fulfillment. To bring a new being into this world, to see its tiny perfection and to dream of its future greatness is the most moving of all experiences and fills one with wonder and exaltation." While part of Indira wanted to focus only on her new family, that was not to be. Her close relationship with her father also meant a close relationship to politics. When he was released from jail, she rushed to see him and left the care of her new baby to relatives. Then, due to bronchitis, she was delayed even further from returning to her boy.

Most biographies of Indira Gandhi portray her children as mere props who led their lives while she rushed around and did important political things. Indira herself was brought up amid busy, chaotic, and very important adult work, and the same was true for her kids. To Indira, however, her children were always central. On parenting, she says,

> **The amount of time spent with children doesn't matter as much as the manner of spending it. When one has only a limited period of time at one's disposal, one naturally makes the most of it. No matter how busy I have been, how tired, or even unwell, I have always taken time off to play or read with my sons. One can teach best by example. Children are extraordinarily perceptive and quick to detect any falsehood or pretence. If they trust and respect you, they will co-operate with you even at a very young age.**

Indeed, motherhood became a metaphor for Indira's feelings for her country, as will be seen in her leadership and campaigning.

Tensions in Indira's marriage surfaced when she decided to serve as hostess for her father in his role as interim prime minister. Leaving Feroze behind, she moved in with her son, Rajiv. In 1946, Indira's second boy was born. The labor was very difficult; she almost died. Jawaharlal Nehru named his grandson Sanjay after the hero of an epic, the Mahabharata. Meanwhile, Indira's estranged husband had begun a pattern of seeing other women.

Indira with her two sons, Rajiv (*left*) and Sanjay (*right*), in London, 1953

A NEW NATION

On August 14, 1947, India achieved its independence, and Indira's father, Pandit Jawaharlal Nehru, became the first prime minister. This was both an ebullient and a turbulent time. India still struggled to hold together disparate religious and cultural groups. There was a mass exodus of Hindus from Pakistan, as well as Muslims from India, and this was not peaceful, but involved massacres, rapes, and other brutalities. Pakistan was divided into western and eastern halves, an awkward geographical arrangement that eventually led to serious conflict.

There are different ways to analyze postcolonial India. To notice only its move toward nationalism is to ignore its numerous groups with their own strong identities. Taking a long view, we could look at

India as the third moment in the great democratic experiment starting with the American and French revolutions. In a way, however, holding together India was hardest of all. Instead of evolving slowly as the other two nations had, India became an independent democracy very suddenly. Within this context India's leaders had to maintain domestic authority and geographic boundaries while providing social opportunities for all of its citizens. That they succeeded as much as they did is truly remarkable.

Still, the road was a rough one from the start. Muslim and Hindu conflicts flared up early on. Indira witnessed a crowd beating up a man whom they took for a Muslim, and she exited her stopped train to rescue him. She then went on to join social workers aiding Muslim refugees, and she met regularly with Mahatma Gandhi to report on her work. Indira's approach was one of rolling up her sleeves, getting in there where the most trouble was, and helping out as productively as she could. She also saw many facets of any given situation and the people involved. In a conversation about this work, she said,

> **You know, we are getting all these people arrested but where is it taking us? It is not helping the situation. We seem to spend all our time with bad people, through trying to find out who is committing these crimes. It is never-ending. Why don't we tackle it in another way? Let us see if there are any people who are not involved in the killing and hatred. Let us try to bring them together.**

And that is indeed what she started to do. Indira continued to check in with Mahatma Gandhi, who was essential to the effort to put down violence against Muslims. Having spoken with Gandhi the day before his assassination, Indira was hit hard by his death. Her description of Gandhi says as much about her as it does about him:

> Each person's understanding of Gandhiji is a measure of his own change and growth. While he was alive many of my age group found it difficult to understand him. Some of us were impatient with what we considered to be his fads, and we found some of his formulations obscure. We took his Mahatmahood for granted, but quarreled with him for bringing mysticism into politics. This applied not only to my generation. . . . Gandhiji himself did not demand unquestioning obedience. He did not want acceptance of his ends and means without a full examination. He encouraged discussion. How many times have I not argued with him, even when a young girl. He regarded no honest opinion as trivial and always found time for those who dissented from him—a quality rare in teachers in our country or in prophets anywhere. . . . To me Gandhiji is a living man who represents the highest level to which a human being can evolve. Steeped in the best from the past he lived in the present, yet for the future. . . . He fashioned his ideas as tools in the course of his experiments in the laboratory of his own life.

TRAVEL AND BUSY SCHEDULES

Jawaharlal Nehru moved into the past residence of the British commander in chief, and Indira joined him with her two boys. Feroze made brief, periodic visits. As happened often in Indira's household, there were extra guests, refugees from struggling or conflicted areas in India. In 1949, Indira suffered a miscarriage, and against doctors' advice, she traveled to the United States with her father.

Upon their return, Indira took on the organization of the festival of dance in New Delhi. She invited tribal dancers from all over India and, along with her father, participated in the dancing. This is when Indira's political profile intensified. She became the chair of the Indian Council for Child Welfare and established a center for underprivileged children in New Delhi.

In 1953, Indira traveled alone to the Soviet Union for the first time as daughter of the prime minister. She was impressed by the friendly reception she received and the work the nation had done to help children. Returning to Russia in 1955 with her father, she was apparently instrumental in easing Nehru and Khrushchev past stalled talks. In gratitude, Khrushchev gave her a mink coat. This came back to haunt her when she took over as India's leader, as the showiness of the gift triggered harsh criticism.

As they traveled extensively around India, Indira and Jawaharlal met with prominent local leaders, social workers, and political activists. Indira had a great memory for names and faces. In 1957, she joined the Central Election Committee but refused a seat in the parliament; instead she opted to work for her father's constituency.

Just as Indira was surrounded by adult activities and concerns as a little girl, so her two sons were surrounded by politics and grown-up tensions. They witnessed their parents' marriage weakening. Their father was the fun parent who came to play with them on weekends. They were then sent off to boarding school while Indira busied herself with her political work.

Indira's marital strife started to take political turns. While Feroze worked to build cases against some of her father's supporters in the Congress Party, Indira, in her new position as president of the Congress Party, also called the Indian National Congress, fought a newly elected Marxist government in Kerala. Feroze was appalled, and

Prime Minister Nehru with Indira, 1955

Jawaharlal also disagreed, arguing that the government that Indira opposed had been elected democratically. But upon the appearance of textbooks using the words of Chinese communist leader Mao Tsetung, Indira argued that brainwashing the youth hurts a democracy. Her thinking here perhaps foreshadowed a controversy that Indira would face much later.

TROUBLE FOR NEHRU

In the late 1950s and early 1960s, Nehru faced some difficulties in both his leadership and his health. Indira stepped in to care for him and operated as his main advisor. In 1959, the Dalai Lama fled Tibet and sought asylum in India. Nehru hesitated, but Indira urged him to welcome the religious leader. Indira also pushed her father to help bring in new leaders to India's government.

Tensions with China increased, partly because of the Dalai Lama, who was considered a threat and traitor by China; that he made his home in India was seen as an affront. Tensions also came from a road the Chinese built in Indian territory without permission. Nehru had tried to negotiate the contentious 2,640-mile (4,249-kilometer) border between China and India with Chou En-lai, the Chinese leader, but this effort was unsuccessful. China invaded quickly and efficiently in October and November 1962, and its soldiers could have gone further, but they stopped as suddenly as they had begun. Chaos ensued, with even the local leadership fleeing the area. It was a humiliating wake-up call for India.

Indira went to the troubled location to help out and to assure the people there that no one had forgotten them. Nehru feared that China would retaliate by kidnapping her. Around this time, Feroze suffered a second heart attack and died at age forty-eight. The couple's two sons were fourteen and sixteen years old. On May 27, 1964, Indira's father, Jawaharlal Nehru, also passed away. Indira had to suffer two huge losses without allowing them to slow her down.

NEW LEADERSHIP

Indira had helped campaign for the Congress Party in the 1962 general election. She spoke of communalism as a dangerous force, opposed to the secularism that her father always had represented. While Indians had always valued and respected their diversity, the geographic division of the states by language, religion, or ethnicity often led to misunderstandings and conflicts. Indira felt secularism was a way to prevent conflict while still respecting individual differences. Said Indira,

> **Communal harmony and the policy of what we call secularism is not against any religion; it respects all religions and stands for the equality for all citizens of India, regardless of their religion or their caste. We give great importance to this policy because we think it is one of the cementing factors of India's unity. Without unity, of course, there can be no stability or progress. A person is less than human when he deprives somebody of his citizens' rights only because of religion.**

Lal Bahadur Shastri became India's next prime minister. He offered the position to Indira, but she refused. Indira later commented, "If I had become PM at that time, they would have destroyed me." Instead, she chose to run the Ministry of Information and Broadcasting, but clearly her involvement was broader than that, and soon enough she would earn the highest position.

With Indira's boys back at boarding school in England, she moved to a quieter, more private residence, yet in the mornings she offered *durbars*, or open house sessions, for peasants, artisans, students, and anyone else who had something to say. She listened respectfully and considered their concerns. When Pakistani forces invaded Kashmir in 1965, Indira went right to the danger and offered support to the troops.

CHAPTER FOUR

Indira Gandhi as Prime Minister

A NOTHER TRAGEDY—SHASTRI'S DEATH from a heart attack—led to an election. This time Indira felt ready. During the transition, Gulzarilal Nanda, an economist and politician, briefly served as an interim prime minister, as he had after Nehru's death. Indira, whose biggest competitor was Morarji Desai, prevailed. Indira was sworn in as the third prime minister of India on January 24, 1966. She called herself a *desh sevika*, or "servant of the nation."

Indira's election coincided with the women's movement in the West, and people worldwide were excited about her. Betty Friedan, the American author of *The Feminine Mystique*, immediately flew to India to write an article about Indira. The new prime minister distanced herself from the Western feminist movement, however, and many Indians viewed her gender as a liability. To Indira, politics was life—her life—and had nothing to do with gender. In an interview with the *New York Times*, she said, "I was brought up to believe that politics is not a career, it is not a job. Politics is certain world trends, where humanity is going, what it is doing. That is what interests me, for politics is the center of everything."

Indira faced plenty of challenges, including infighting in her party and government. The old guard was suspicious of her, and perhaps disappointed that she wasn't as malleable as they had hoped, and they put up stumbling blocks to prevent newer, younger members from getting involved. Indira faced drought, famine, food shortages, and riots. Language and cultural groups clashed, with speakers of Punjabi fighting for

Indira Gandhi, newly elected prime minister of India, January 18, 1966

independence. When she allowed for a separate state, people speaking the Hindi language revolted. She then established a separate Hindu state called Haryana. As had become typical of her reactions to strife, Indira went directly to the troubled area to try to ease the conflict. This was a very difficult time for Indira, with such large national crises and awkward, angry government meetings. Her confidence was shaken.

CONFIDENCE IS KEY

It was important for Indira to appear strong and confident as she embarked on her first visit to the United States as prime minister, with a stopover in France on the way. While seeking aid for India's food shortage, Indira was determined, then and forever after, not to

U.S. president Lyndon Johnson and his wife, Lady Bird, with Indira Gandhi (*right*), 1966

be beholden to any nation—not to beg—but she bargained over the devaluing of the rupee in exchange for the aid from the United States that India so sorely needed. While some people criticized her for this, her goal was for India to achieve a "green revolution" and to become self-sufficient with food within three years. While this did not play out exactly as intended, India's success surpassed similar efforts in other developing nations.

Indira's confidence was growing as her dedication to serve her country remained constant. With this new strength, she also proved herself willing to make an unpopular decision. A good leader, a strong leader, is not always popular. Some people felt that Indira's commitment to Swadeshi (self-reliance) hurt India's economy. Indira wanted her country to remain strong and not rely on anyone else. India had so recently become an independent nation in the first place. Still, this independent spirit caused tensions with the United States throughout many negotiations. Like other world leaders, Indira tried to achieve a delicate balance between appearing strong and being willing to negotiate and compromise.

In 1969, two years after the devaluation of the rupee, Indira said, "The public sector was conceived as the base of Indian industry so that the country might have more machines, more steel. It also ensured India's freedom. To the extent India depended on imports its independence was compromised." Like all of her highly politicized family members, Indira was passionate about her beliefs, sometimes to the degree of being inflexible. She was able to accept aid from the United States without feeling beholden, while she could accept the devaluation move as simply part of the deal. Even though not all of her actions succeeded, she was becoming more self-assured. And she stayed true to some of her basic beliefs and reasons behind accepting the position of prime minister in the first place.

The first major address that Indira offered as prime minister, at India's Independence Day on August 15, 1966, was strong, passionate, and eloquent. The 1967 general election showed Indira's strength and charisma. She was an awesome campaigner, reaching out directly to the people. She traveled 15,000 miles (24,140 kilometers) all over India and spoke at hundreds of public meetings. Using folksy and sympathetic words, she appealed to people from humble backgrounds. By appearing both regal and homey, she attracted huge crowds and tremendous support.

Indira came into her own as she worked against some derogatory comments about her gender. According to Katherine Frank, journalists referred to her as "the little woman"; her political rival, Morarji Desai, once called her "this mere *chikri*" ("slip of a girl"); and there were other negative remarks. She turned that negativity around in a speech in which she talked about taking care of her "family" (the Indian people), which was composed of many different castes and religions that often fought among themselves. After this speech, she earned the title Mother Indira. Here we see the metaphor of motherhood playing out, as her gender represented a source of strength.

Even so, Indira had detractors throughout her long tenure as prime minister. When she nationalized banks, many people rejoiced, but some grumbled. Her longtime rival, Morarji Desai, whom she had appeased by appointing finance minister, resigned from her cabinet. Chafing at being Indira's deputy, he disagreed vehemently with her on key issues. He never could accept being the older, more experienced politician and yet answering to her. She stubbornly pushed back whenever she could—for example, by appointing her cabinet without consulting him or anyone else. Relations with the United States were never smooth. For one thing, Indira did not show the support for Israel or the disapproval of nearby Arab nations that

American leaders expected of her. That, combined with U.S. activity in Vietnam, made her suspicious that Asia would be squeezed in, with India right in the middle. Sometimes Indira's way of showing disapproval was to be silent. This often infuriated her opponents.

Indira developed two strategies for dealing with tension and strife. When facing mixed alliances and infighting in the legislature, she would reach out to the people and call on a direct relationship with them. In troubling times, she withdrew mentally, almost as if she were meditating. She once spoke of a void, such as those found in space, that existed inside people:

You can retire into [the voids] without disrupting yourself. . . . [T]hat is why you can't get tired because you are automatically relaxing yourself.

Her withdrawal contributed to her often appearing aloof, although she used this strategy sparingly. When speaking publicly or spending time with her family, she was fully present.

THE FAMILY GROWS, TROUBLE BREWS

In 1968, Rajiv married Sonia Maino, a young, Italian, Catholic woman whom he had met at Cambridge University in England. While Indira easily accepted a foreign daughter-in-law, Sonia's father was opposed to the relationship from the start. Indira welcomed the new couple into her home and apparently grew quite attached to Sonia. Indira did not have many close friends. Katherine Frank lists only three: Dorothy Norman, Marie Seton, and Pupul Jayakar (author

The wedding eve ceremony, with Indira (*right*), bride-to-be, Sonia Maino (*left*), groom-to-be, Rajiv, and Sonia Maino's mother, Paola, February 24, 1968

of *Indira Gandhi: An Intimate Biography*). Thus, her friendship with Sonia was significant for all concerned. Sanjay was back home too at this time, so Indira's family life was full.

Meanwhile, the conflicts in the government remained. Internal bickering continued, especially after the sudden death of Indira's choice for president, Zakir Hussain. Some say Indira's policies were merely strategies for self-preservation. Says Frank, "Frequently in Indira's political life, ideological and self-serving initiatives overlapped. For her biographer, once Indira is established as Prime Minister, her behavior—both political and personal—becomes increasingly ambiguous and open to interpretation." In other words, Indira's motives were complex and almost impossible to understand with certainty. It is difficult for politicians to avoid such ambiguity, because their jobs are always twofold: to maintain one's power and to serve the people.

The beginnings of a long, devastating chain of trouble with Sanjay appeared when Indira helped him secure a license to produce a small, cheap, Indian car—a version of Germany's Volkswagen. He passed over other car companies with vastly more experience, such as Toyota and Renault. This was Sanjay's first taste of power and favoritism, which he was to make the most of for years to come. As Frank tells it, ever since Sanjay's father had died, he had had a weird hold on his mother. Some speculated that guilt drove Indira to spoil her son, as Sanjay had accused his mother of causing his father's death because of her estrangement from him.

Grown sons, Rajiv and Sanjay, with their mother, Indira, on the grounds of their home in Delhi, 1967

VICTORY AND HARD WORK

In 1970, Indira approved India's first nuclear power plant, which brought much pride to the nation. Indira experienced personal pride and joy, as well, with the birth of her first grandchild, Rajiv's son. Her reelection in 1971 proved her popularity and success, but it occurred after many struggles within the government. At one point, there were actually two simultaneous meetings of the legislature—one at the regular place and one in Indira's home. Her opponents tried to dismiss her from the party. Indira prevailed. Apparently this split was another significant assertion of her strength, because opposition groups that traditionally remained a part of the Congress Party were ousted. The *New York Times* praised Indira: "She has proved herself a courageous, tough-minded politician as well as an exceedingly skilful tactician—a Prime Minister in her own right and not a transitional figure, trading on her legacy as the daughter of Nehru."

The election was a difficult fight. Going right to the people, Indira campaigned widely and reached out to a range of constituencies. The motto of her opponents was "Remove Indira," while her motto was "Remove Poverty." Still, Indira tended to run on her personality and her mothering presence, not so much on issues. When a *Newsweek* reporter asked her what the issues were in the election, she said, "I am the issue." Because the election was all about her, her victory offered further consolidation of her power. The prime minister's position was stronger than ever before. Voters reported that they were voting for her, not for her party. This made some people, especially her opponents, uneasy. If she was seen as winning by personality instead of platform, this was seen as a dangerous neglecting of important issues and also possibly allowing too much power for the one personality, Indira Gandhi.

Indira never had time to rejoice in a victory, as she could not ignore the unrest in Pakistan. Free elections had not gone the way President Yahya Khan had predicted, and his crackdown on Eastern Pakistan was appalling. Soldiers slaughtered both Hindu and Muslim people. Many refugees sought safety in India. After getting support for them through the legislature, Indira went to the refugee camps. Asserting that this was an international crisis, she held off from immediately recognizing Eastern Pakistan as an independent state (soon it would become Bangladesh).

U.S. leaders were conflicted about Pakistan; the people, alarmed by the massacres, demanded justice, while President Nixon wanted to ally himself with Khan partly to help with negotiations with China. Indira and Nixon did not seem to like or trust one another. During their negotiations, Nixon apparently demanded an answer to a proposal that Indira had said she would think about but then had ignored. Later, in another battle of wills, Nixon sent a fleet to linger in Indian waters, as a gesture of American might, but Indira refused to be bullied. She remained firm in her support of Eastern Pakistan.

Later, in an interview by the *Washington Post*, Indira was asked how she could handle such pressure as with the war with Pakistan. She referred to her Hindu philosophy: being a realist and taking things as they come. She said she didn't

Indira Gandhi and U.S. president Richard Nixon in Washington, D.C., November 4, 1971

like small talk. The reporter asked how she could race around the country, doing all that she did, and then be "fresh as a daisy and totally relaxed" for an interview the next day. She replied obliquely and with composure that it was because she was an Indian. Then the interviewer commented, "I can see why you got on Nixon's nerves." Both Indira and the American interviewer acknowledged that Indira's culture was key to who she was: a competent, unflappable leader who moves through any situation with grace and equanimity. This could be maddening to anyone who did not have such self-control and self-composure.

MORE SUCCESS: FOR BANGLADESH AND INDIRA

In spite of the pressure from American's 7th Fleet closing in, Indira held her ground, and Bangladesh was liberated. This was a huge victory for Indira. It legitimized her strength and determination as a leader and her unflinching commitment to India's power and autonomy. She could have pushed further with aggression against Pakistan, but instead she spoke of balance and friendship. Her opponents were not happy about this. To them, she replied,

> All I know is that I must fight for peace and I must take those steps which will lead us to peace. If they do not work out, we are prepared. Had we stood up saying as when two children are quarreling, 'You have taken my toy. I must have it before I speak to you,' or something like that, if we had that kind of attitude what would have happened? The time has come when Asia must wake up to its destiny, must wake up to the real needs of its people.
> We must stop fighting among ourselves, no matter what our previous quarrels, no matter what the previous hatred and bitterness.
> The time has come today when we must bury the past.

Overall, this was the peak of Indira's power. Somehow she had combined patriotism with radicalism, had remained strong in the face of huge challenges, and had managed on her own to broker a very difficult peace with Pakistan. (In the final moment Zulfikar Ali Bhutto of Pakistan had asked the advisors to leave, and just he and Indira had carried out the final discussions.) She had won over the political right, center, and left. As one journalist, Kuldip Nayar, pointed out, Indira had "[w]on the war and she appeared to have also won the peace. She was the undisputed leader of the country; the cynicism of the intellectuals had given way to admiration; the masses were even more worshipful. . . . She was hailed as the greatest leader India had ever had."

Indira also offered leadership on the environment. In 1972 she delivered the keynote address at the United Nations Conference on the Human Environment. She was one of the first heads

Indira (*right*), after talks with Pakistani president Zulfikar Ali Bhutto (second from left), July 3, 1972. Bhutto's daughter Benazir is on the left.

of state to see nature and the biosphere as global issues of great importance. She said, "[P]rogress is becoming synonymous with an assault on nature."

BAD SIGNS

Even while Indira was at her peak, the beginnings of the unraveling of her power and influence were in place. She had always had detractors, and the Congress Party had always been an uncomfortable arrangement of disparate interests. After the victory with Pakistan, however, some critics found her arrogant. Others objected to the power she gave to her son Sanjay, who seemed to be incompetent and corrupt. Some of Indira's most controversial measures had the support, if not the direct leadership, of Sanjay. In addition, the year 1973 brought drought, a huge increase in oil prices, inflation, labor strikes, and general unrest.

Indira became more and more secretive and suspicious. Sanjay was one of the only people she felt she could trust. People were forming new coalitions against her, and there were threats of kidnapping legislators' children. Indira held back on responding. Violence broke out. Some people were killed, many more were hurt, and thousands were arrested. A huge railroad strike followed, and it threatened to shut down the country. Without transportation of food supplies, people would starve. Indira did act on this. She arrested instigators or threw them out of government housing. Her actions created confusion and bitterness.

Indira was also starting to control the state governments. She would pick chief ministers loyal to her and get rid of disloyal ministers through what was called president's rule. She began to suspend state legislatures as a way to freeze out opposition to the Congress Party in those states.

As Indira centralized power, the Congress Party showed signs of corruption. Politicians saw their positions as a means toward wealth and status rather than a form of public service; while many Congress Party members still dressed in the homespun cloth, their wives flouted luxurious, non-Indian attire and accessories. Indira herself continued to live with austerity and simplicity, however. As part of her no-nonsense attitude, she campaigned to eliminate dowries, a tradition she felt was humiliating and demeaning for women. This was a huge step for women's rights. Although Indira did not necessarily consider herself a feminist, she was always an advocate for women and children. She pushed through a constitutional amendment that removed land concessions given to the princes, or maharajas, when the nation was born. Indira needed public support, but she did not compromise her beliefs in order to be liked.

Still, the complicated politics started to depress Indira, who was feeling trapped, too busy for introspection. It seemed she was somehow losing her balance. In addition to other stresses, 1974 was the third year in a row of drought and food shortages. While Indira did not have time for any kind of private life, events presented themselves. For example, Sanjay married Maneka Anand, a boisterous Sikh woman only nineteen years old. Indira offered generous gifts and welcomed the new couple to her home, but her new daughter-in-law did not fit in well and was often loud, disrespectful, and willful.

CHAPTER FIVE

Emergency

INALLY, IN 1975, THE ANTI-INDIRA FORCES were successful in unseating her. Due to a technicality in the election process, she was barred from public office for six years. An opponent accused her of using government resources for campaigning, and the court ordered her to give up her seat in India's parliament. This effectively removed Indira from office because the prime minister is required to serve on either the Lok Sabha (Lower House) or the Rajya Sabha (Upper House). People expected Indira to resign, but instead she ordered the arrests of opposition leaders, including some who were quite popular. People with sympathetic views of Indira pointed out that the broiling plots within government had left her all alone.

Distressed by what he saw as India losing its way, Jayaprakash Narayan, an old Nehru and Gandhi supporter, built up an opposition political movement. He developed a large following. With that, on top of the chaos and unrest, Indira started to worry about conspiracies, perhaps even ones instigated by the Central Intelligence Agency (CIA) in the United States. She believed that if she fell from power, India would not survive. She felt only drastic measures would save the situation. Emmanuel Pouchepadass, a writer who presents Indira's story through her own words from extensive interviews, talks

Indira at her home as demonstrators protest outside, June 14, 1975 of mediocre, ambitious, self-serving politicians who backed Indira when it was convenient and betrayed her when she was out of favor:

> **She was highly superior to them and her sensitivity, always on the alert, made her discover that she was alone. It is hardly astonishing that she could only find moral support and unwavering backing from her son.**

Indira received huge amounts of support from world leaders and average citizens, and her family convinced her not to resign. This is when she started to develop a plan for a highly controversial state of emergency, which she called Disciplined Democracy. Indira implemented her plan on June 26, 1975. It disappointed many people, changed her reputation forever, and to this day still evokes ambivalence and discomfort in those who analyze it. At the time, however, very few people directly confronted Indira with their displeasure, and both houses of the parliament endorsed the plan. Her son Sanjay had a lot of say in arrests and targets of censorship.

The level of press censorship under Indira's plan was alarming. Ironically, however, it was Indira's dedication to democracy that compelled her to instigate this legislation. She seemed to feel that the ends justified the means. Indira cared deeply about what she thought was best for her country, and she felt that even extreme measures were justified. In a speech of June 27, 1975, she explained, "A climate of violence and hatred had been created which resulted in the assassination of a Cabinet Minister and an attempt on the life of the Chief Justice. . . . The kind of programme envisaged by some of the Opposition group is not compatible with democracy, it is anti-national by any test and could not be allowed. Since the proclamation of emergency the whole country has gone back to normal except for partial hartal, and minor incidents in Gujarat. This sense of normalcy must be maintained. And there should be realization that even in a democracy there are limits which cannot be crossed. Violent action and senseless satyagrahas will pull down the whole edifice which has been built over the years with such labour and hope. . . . You know that I have always believed in freedom of the press and I still do, but like all freedoms it has to be exercised with responsibility and restraint. . . . Sometimes several newspapers have deliberately distorted news and made malicious and provocative comments. . . . The purpose of censorship is to restore a climate of trust. . . . This is the time for unity and discipline. I am fully confident that with each day, the situation will improve and that in this task our people in towns and villages will give us their full support so that the country will be strengthened."

To say that censorship leads to trust, or that a democracy has limits and excessive disruption must be controlled in any way possible, seems paradoxical and perhaps hard to understand. However, most democratic nations, including the United States, have suffered under leaders who seemed to feel this way. Indira Gandhi was coming from perhaps a different tradition, from a new, self-described democracy that seemed mainly pragmatic. Whatever worked—whatever strategy could unite an incredibly diverse nation and keep it running smoothly—was acceptable. But many people objected to Indira's decision and even felt betrayed by it.

In an attempt to offer a clear, positive view ahead, Indira put forth her 20 Point Program in simple language that all could understand.

The economy improved. She banned fundamentalist, far right, and extreme religious political parties. She felt that the factions working against her were ultimately bad for the country and bad for democracy.

Apparently what got more attention and ultimately caused more damage was Sanjay's 5 Point Plan. Indira's son had entered politics through a back door. He wielded power that he hadn't earned, and no one had put him in his place. Some say that his mother was afraid of him. His two biggest mistakes were the slum clearance and sterilization programs. The former lead to widespread destruction of homes; thousands of poor people were uprooted, and many were injured as they protested this indignity. The sterilization program was designed to relieve India's overpopulation. In Indian culture, however, having children is connected to a person's self-worth. Children are highly valued, and they are expected to earn money and to support their families. Sterilization could only go through if imposed from the top, which the state of emergency allowed. Sanjay's methods were harsh. He instituted a quota requiring that government employees achieve a certain amount of sterilization procedures before getting paid. Some people were even forced into the operation. For example, homeless people were arrested for vagrancy and then brought to sterilization clinics.

DAMAGE CONTROL

Indira postponed elections and extended the state of emergency twice, apparently at Sanjay's urging. Some argue that the second time was a mistake; if there had still been enough support for the second extension, the Congress Party could have won the election and thus justified her actions. Without that justification, she was more open to criticism. Indira became increasingly uncomfortable with the delay, and in 1977 she changed her mind and announced elections after all. She was able to defy her younger son twice—first, with this move, and second, by ordering the release of many political prisoners and lifting the press censorship guidelines.

Ironically, just before Indira declared the state of emergency, writer Henry Christman said the following about Indira Gandhi:

> That Indian democracy has survived to this point of history is due in large part to Prime Minster Indira Gandhi, who has had the foresight to recognize the economic, social and political problems that could bring about the collapse of her country, and has endeavored to meet and solve those problems within the structure of parliamentary democracy.

Christman goes on to quote Trevor Drieberg's biography of Indira:

> . . . she could do without the party, she has achieved this by purely democratic, parliamentary processes. . . . she is there by the people's unfettered will, expressed through free elections. She is a political phenomenon, in a class by herself. Her sanction is the people. Their votes put her in power despite the attempts of various elite groups to see that she was shut out of its portals.

India is an incredibly diverse nation with a wide range of languages and religious affiliations. Because of this, suggests writer Edward Luce, an independent India needs to be a democratic India. The most puzzling and disturbing moment in Indira's career, then, was the state of emergency, under which she asserted autocratic rule. Surprisingly, many Western leaders supported her decision. She did manage to restore a federal democracy, which allowed a peaceful outlet for all of the many regional interests. Was she right? For many, no. Her actions were seen as a betrayal of all that India had fought for, even though it was her passionate commitment to democracy and India's autonomy that made her desperate enough to pursue that course. Here is what Indira Gandhi has to say about democracy:

> **I believe in democracy not as democracy but because I believe in the individual. Under democracy the individual gets more rights than he does under any other system. He has greater opportunity for development. Moreover, in a country of India's size and variety, one has to make allowances for small explosions in order to avoid a big one. . . . Resorting every now and then to the so-called ultimate weapon of Satyagraha is not democracy, nor is forcing, through intimidation, coercion, duly elected legislators to resign. Democracy comprises freedom of expression and debate, but can a systematic and virulent character assassination without any factual basis be indulged in the name of democracy?**

Indira's description of democracy as offering individual freedoms, but not complete freedom of the press, is puzzling. *Satyagraha*, a term and action developed by Mohandas Gandhi, contributed to the independence movement that finally earned India its freedom from British rule. Yet according to Indira, others later misapplied and abused his concept simply to cause unrest. Does a political leader have the right to decide when the press is abusing its freedom or reporting irresponsibly? Indira seemed to think so. She felt that the buildup of plots against her, as well as protests against the government, were leading to chaos that would damage the entire country. Was she merely protecting her own power through whatever means it took? Said Indira, "The Government's responsibility is not to brainwash people, nor to lead them in one direction, but to allow them to grow. It also is its responsibility to see that nothing happens which will destroy the very basis of the country, its unity, its integrity, its stability or its strength."

Katherine Frank assesses Indira's state of emergency declaration in this way:

> It is possible that Indira also had genuine qualms about extending the Emergency and violating any longer the constitution and the form of government her father had devoted his life to creating. For Indira, the Emergency had been a means to an end. But she was no Bhutto or Mujib. For all her failings and despite her irrational belief that only she could lead and control the country, on some level she remained committed to democracy. She was guilty of hubris but not megalomania.

Pupul Jayakar offers an interesting analysis of Indira at this time. According to Jayakar, Indira had always been able to take a step back from difficult situations and let an answer come to her. She had an uncanny ability to deliver action with perfect timing that often caught her opponents off-guard, but somehow, at this time, she lost that ability. She acted in a trapped, impulsive manner. After the emergency, when she heard news of many abuses that she had not known about, her deepest sadness was having become so distanced from her people. Perhaps she never recovered that balance and equanimity again.

OUT OF WORK

Indira was indeed taking a risk in calling the next elections. No authoritarian leader has ever given up power or allowed a legitimate vote the way Indira Gandhi did. She had no way of knowing how it would turn out, with all of the tumult and unrest. She certainly could not have predicted that Jagjivan Ram, the minister of irrigation and agriculture, would resign, defect from the Congress Party, found a new party, and then join with the opposition Janata Party. It was then that he chose to denounce both Indira and the state of emergency. Indira and her party lost. She resigned, and was suddenly not only without a job, but also without a home.

A friend gave Indira a place to stay, and she moved her whole family into the smaller quarters. She lost all of her staff. While out of politics, Indira never sat idle. One of her projects was investigating the potential of computers and computer literacy. She called in a foreign expert for consultation.

On March 23, 1977, Indira's longtime rival, Morarji Desai, became the fourth prime minister of India. His Janata Party was perhaps more fractured than the Congress Party. They had united through distaste for Indira Gandhi, and she seemed to be the only issue they could agree upon, so instead of getting the country back in shape, they focused on bringing Indira and Sanjay to justice. Many other Indians took up this obsession as well. Indira and her family were followed and wiretapped. The media released all sorts of anti-Indira texts, and it became intellectually trendy to bash her.

Amidst this fracas, landowners in the remote village of Belchi massacred a large number of Dalits ("untouchables"). The new government failed to respond, but Indira immediately went there, even though it was a dangerous area with free-roaming robbers and she no longer had any security staff. After dealing with flooded roads, transport by tractor, and an elephant ride across a raging river, Indira arrived, and grateful crowds greeted her. She visited and made amends with Narayan, who had retired in nearby Patna, the capital of that region, and took another big risk by visiting her constituency— the very people who had just voted her down. She spoke to huge, receptive crowds and apologized for the emergency. As the Shah

Commission was preparing to put Indira and Sanjay on trial, she once again had transcended governmental procedures by appealing directly to the people.

INDIRA PREVAILS

While Indira did end up being arrested, the judge immediately dismissed the minor charges. She ended up as the wronged victim, while the Janata Party looked like the bad guys. The Shah Commission fizzled out. Indira was back in politics, although she held only half of the newly split Congress Party. Her half was called Congress I (*I* stood for Indira). Each party had a visual icon, so people who were illiterate could still vote. Indira lost the symbol previously associated with her party—the cow with a calf—but that may have been for the best, as many people associated the symbol with her and Sanjay. Instead, her half of the party adopted a raised, open hand representing benediction, blessings, and grace. This symbol is still in use today.

Indira chose the candidate for her party, a Muslim woman named Mohsina Kidwai. Their campaign appealed to the poor and disenfranchised and women, many of whom went against the advice of husbands or other advisors in their support of the Congress (I) Party.

As Indira campaigned and gained popularity, the new government backed down on trying to prosecute or jail her, even though the Shah Commission finally produced a report condemning her and her government for all sorts of abuses during the state of emergency and identifying flawed reasons for declaring the emergency in the first place. The document was awkward, written in wordy "legalese," and did not cause the stir that its supporters had hoped. Indira was off-limits, but Sanjay was not. He was arrested and jailed for one month.

CHAPTER SIX

Beginnings
and Endings

ACCORDING TO SOME ANALYSTS, THE DEEP divisions across India in 1980 were the direct results of Indira's leadership—namely, her centralizing of power and the resulting loss of autonomy for individual states— yet many people perceived her as the only one who could save the country. She campaigned so tirelessly and extensively that one in every four voters heard her speak. She won two constituencies (Indian law allows candidates to run for more than one), and her party was successful all over the country. Even her son, Sanjay, won and finally earned a legitimate place in the government. On January 14, 1980, Indira was sworn in as prime minister for the fourth time. Unlike leaders of the Janata Party, she had no interest in seeking vengeance against those who had tried to humiliate and defeat her.

TOO MUCH SADNESS

Soon after Indira's victory, she faced the sudden death of her younger son, Sanjay, in a plane crash. Apparently he had been attempting a loop in a private plane but had lost control. While the whole country grieved and elevated him to martyr status— thus conveniently forgetting all of the charges and suspicions against him—Indira seemed to fall apart slowly. Those who saw her as a shrewd politician to the end viewed her actions as smart and strategic, but others noted some desperation and loss of confidence. She relied more and more on a trusted guru, behaved in

A joyous moment after election victory; Indira at her New Delhi residence November 9, 1978 a reactive way, and played one group—a caste, religious, or political group—off of another in order to further her own agenda.

The guru with whom Indira had aligned herself was allegedly corrupt and taking advantage of her. That is not to say that all astrologers and spiritual advisors were off base or not worth her attention. Jayakar reports that just after Sanjay was born, one seer said that Sanjay had inherited an ancestor's inability to discriminate between right and wrong, and that results would be much more important to him than how he achieved them. In 1980 another seer foretold great sorrow facing Indira in that coming year—which ended up being the year of Sanjay's death.

Unrest continued, especially in Punjab. For a long time the Sikhs and the Hindus in this region had gotten along fine and even had intermarried. Recently, however, a local Sikh leader named Bhindranwale had gained power and popularity and had led violent attacks against Hindus and their temples while pushing for an independent state. Religious conflict continued throughout India, and there were attacks against Dalits. Some Dalits converted to Islam or Christianity in the desperate hope of keeping safe, but the discrimination continued. Bhindranwale called for a protest of the Asian Games, a huge expense that seemed to be diverting funds from much-needed areas, and in the police response, many innocent Sikhs were harassed. Attempts at negotiating with Bhindranwale failed. The crisis would soon reach tragic proportions.

The 1983 state assembly elections were disastrous on several levels. The Congress Party lost to movie stars with no political experience. Indira became anguished as she watched her party unravel. In a letter she commented, "Winning and losing are part of democracy and one takes them in one's stride. But in India there is a bitterness and vindictiveness." She went on to complain about shallow people making uninformed decisions, superficial alliances, and easy betrayals.

In addition, ongoing unrest in the state of Assam had finally built up to terrible proportions. Many long-term residents had been disgruntled with the area's Bengali immigrants, partly because they were easy Congress Party votes. The Assamese movement was backed by both the Janata Party and the Hindu Bharatiya Janata Party, ongoing adversaries of Indira's. They pushed to boycott the elections. Violence broke out. Hindus and Muslims alike murdered Bengalis, including innocent women and children. Indira went to the area and was overwhelmed by what she found. She could not find the words to describe the horror.

These were tumultuous times. A growing middle class fell prey to consumerism and the race for status symbols. The population growth was putting increasing pressure on limited resources. Poor people moved toward cities in search of better lives and often landed in slums. The tensions between villages and cities increased. The emerging generation knew nothing of India's struggle for freedom. People seemed to approve of anything new in the arts and in other areas of society. Indira saw all of this and was determined not to give in to a divided India.

Amazingly, amid the busiest times, Indira managed to pursue questions about self-knowledge and spirituality with her friend Pupul Jayakar. She interacted with artists, read, went to exhibits, and enjoyed music. Politics involved all of life, and all aspects of life were important to her. She found her own way to pursue silence and peace as she tried to maintain her composure and her endless energy.

HER ENERGY DOES NOT DIMINISH

Indira started to complain to her friends of the closed minds of foreign leaders. She felt the need to reach out directly to people on an international level, much as she had always done at home. She began

THE MUSIC OF INDIA

Indira Gandhi had a deep love for Indian arts and music. Her country's music has a long and rich history. From the very beginning, it reflected the mixture of religions and traditions that make up India. Its basis is sangeet, a combination of three art forms: vocal music, instrumental music, and dance. While unified in the past, the three forms have branched out and developed into separate, specialized arts as well.

More contemporary classical Indian music is based on two main concepts: *raga*, which means "melody" or "mood," and *tal*, which is the rhythm. While this underlying theory affects all of Indian music, there are regional differences and a rich, complex heritage, from folk and religious pasts and a range of cultures.

India has many unique musical instruments. The best known are the sitar, a stringed instrument, and the tabla, a kind of drum.

India also has its own popular music. *Filmi* are songs that come from musical movies, many of which are big productions made in Bollywood (a cross of *Bombay* and *Hollywood*). A lot of the popular music remains true to India's folk and classical heritage.

to build cultural bridges, such as bringing a "festival of India" to England and the United States. The festival was a huge success that helped with U.S relations. It was her first official visit to the United States in eleven years. Reagan was the president who greeted her this time, and while she found him perfectly cordial, she was disappointed to discover what she described as a limited attention span for serious issues, such as nuclear disarmament. He would quickly change the subject to lighter matters.

To the public, Indira seemed to be handling crises well. She was getting good press. She chaired an international nonalignment committee meeting. Indira upheld her father's policy of nonalignment even more forcefully than he had. To her, maintaining India's hard-earned independence meant depending on no other nation:

> So far as the West is concerned, it seems to us that nothing we do can be right. Because they would like us to do things which would keep us beholden to them. Because we are saying we want to be independent. Young people don't remember this, but the worst part of being under foreign rule was the constant humiliation. Going to jail or being beaten up was a very small part of our suffering. The really galling part was that you were constantly being humiliated in your own country.

Indira also hosted a ceremony of Commonwealth heads of government. She appeared cool, gracious, and regal. Meanwhile, another ongoing problem resurfaced: Punjab.

Violence had been continuing, largely due to Bhindranwale and his followers in the separatist movement, but it got more attention

Indira in Washington D.C., with President Ronald Reagan

with the murder of a police chief named A. S. Atwal, a prominent Sikh who did not support the separatist movement. The chief minister of the Punjab asked Indira to allow him to send police into the temple that Bhindranwale had made his headquarters. Indira refused, perhaps partly on the advice of someone who had a bone to pick with that minister, and partly because a divided Sikh population benefited her party. Other advisors warned her strongly against this decision. According to Katherine Frank, " . . . by now Indira had not only lost her political judgment but also any vestiges of her old uncanny sense of timing and decisiveness." Meanwhile, Bhindranwale built up stronger forces with more weapons.

THE PROBLEM LEADS TO TRAGEDY

The situation got worse, with failing negotiations, mounting violence, and threats that grain would be blocked from exiting the Punjab, which was a major food source for the entire country. At this point, Indira had to resort to force. Many Indian soldiers—and innocent people—lost their lives. Despite a mandate that the soldiers not damage the temple to which Bhindranwale had retreated, this holy site was almost completely destroyed in the process of killing the separatist leader. The soldiers also destroyed a sacred library that the writer Wolpert calls the "Vatican or Mecca of the Sikh faith." Wolpert questioned, "Why had [Indira] opted for what clearly seems now to have been tantamount to signing her own death warrant?"

Indira knew how bad this destruction looked, and she started to talk with her family about her own death; she even wrote out instructions for her funeral. She also worried obsessively about her family members, yet she kept up appearances—Indira worked, ate,

INDIA'S DIVERSITY OF FAITHS

Ironically, the Sikh religion, a relatively new one, was founded with thoughts of harmony between Hinduism and Islam. Its spiritual leaders pulled monotheism from Islam and reincarnation and karma from Hinduism. The religion downplays ritual and worship and emphasizes the presence of God within each person. This group includes a little less than 2 percent of India's population.

Two ancient belief systems, Vedic and Shraman, led to the variety of Sikhism that we know today. Vedic eventually developed into Hinduism, and Shraman branched into Buddhism and Jainism.

Hinduism goes way back to what is called the Vedantic period, around the second century CE, but its roots existed as long ago as 4000 to 2200 BCE. This religion has its own branches and complexities. Hinduism's founding beliefs may have come partly from aborigines in the newly agricultural society. These basic principles have remained in place: reincarnation (the main self or soul is reborn in a new form), samsara (the cycle of birth, death, and rebirth), karma (the deeds that one performs in one life impact the next one), and moksha (freedom from samsara, granted to good souls).

Two main principles of Hinduism are Dhama (ethics and duties) and yoga (paths or practices). There is no one holy book, but the important founding texts are the Upanishads. A collection of texts called the Puranas includes myths with many gods and goddesses who behave like humans, not unlike the ancient Greek and Roman traditions. The two most important epics of Hinduism are the Mahabharata and the Ramayana. There have been many splinter groups and different sects within the Hindu faith. Overall, Hinduism represents 80.4 percent of India's population.

Islam, a monotheistic religion, follows the leader Muhammad. Devout Muslims offer prayers five times a day, at prescribed times. According to a census of 2001, Islam comprises 13.4 percent of India's population. About 80 percent of Indian Muslims practice Sunni Islam. What differentiates Indian Islam from the practice of other nations is its emphasis on shrines to Sufi saints, who were known for spreading the message of peace and universal love.

Buddhism, sometimes called a philosophy instead of religion because followers do not worship a god, represents 0.7 percent of India's population. Another nontheistic religion of India is Jainism, whose followers invoke divine principles but do not worship a god. These believers make up 0.5 percent of the population.

Much smaller segments of the population belong to other religions, including Zoroastrianism, Judaism, Christianity, some tribal religions, and the Baha'i Faith, which in India has the largest following in the world, at about 2 million.

Religion is very important to most Indian citizens, many of whom carry out rituals daily. Many Indians' eating habits come from spiritual beliefs. For instance, both Buddhism and Jainism require vegetarianism. Hinduism bans beef, and Islam prohibits pork. Religion also impacts the nation's politics, particularly when two or more groups are not getting along or are vying for power or property. Some analysts argue that British rule deepened religious divisions, particularly between Hindus and Muslims. The caste system, associated with Hinduism, drove some people from the lower castes to Christianity and Buddhism. Because of India's commitment to freedom of religion, none of the holidays of any of the faiths have been declared national holidays.

and carried out her days as if the fiasco in the Punjab had never occurred. Those around her worried, and the head of the Intelligence Bureau ordered that all Sikh security men on duty at her residence be asked to leave. Indira insisted that India was secular and vetoed the order.

In these ominous days, Indira wrote a note that was later found in her home. It was a heartbreaking, heartfelt message:

> If I die a violent death as some fear and a few are plotting, I know the violence will be in the thought and the action of the assassin, not in my dying—for no hate is dark enough to overshadow the extent of my love for my people and my country; no force is strong enough to divert me from my purpose and my endeavour to take this country forward. A poet has written of love—'how can I feel humble with the wealth of you beside me.' I can say the same of India. I cannot understand how anyone can be an Indian and not be proud—the richness and infinite variety of our composite heritage, the magnificence of the people's spirit, equal to any disaster or burden, firm in their faith . . . even in poverty and hardship.

On October 31, 1984, as Indira was leaving her home to start her day, two of her guards shot and killed her. They were both Sikh. She had known one of them since 1980. The other was new. After the assassination, the first guard, Beant Singh, was heard to say in Punjabi, "I have done what I had to do. Now you do what you have to do."

Indira's son, Rajiv, was chosen to be the next prime minister. Nearly everyone except his wife, Sonia, was in favor of this. Indira's ashes were scattered over the Himalayas, as she had requested.

She had chosen to rest in Kashmir, her birthplace. At the place of her cremation stands a 15-foot-high (4.5-m-high) weathered rock of jasper with veins of iron ore.

Pupul Jayakar, her loyal friend and biographer, says this of Indira Gandhi:

> A woman so closely tuned to the country, so complex, so skillful, so far-seeing, so capable of an insightful listening, moved by beauty; and yet, at times, so obsessive, ruthless, brittle, even trivial—a woman who refused to be measured, who laid her own ground rules. She loved her country with passion and tenderness, like a tigress guarding her cubs; her antennae would awaken at the slightest threat. She never ceased to regard herself as a guardian of India and its frontiers.

Indira's family gathers at the cremation pyre, November 3, 1984.

KEEP AN EYE ON THE NEWS

Many of the themes, conflicts, and personalities surrounding Indira continue to play important roles in India. In an opinion piece in the *New York Times* on December, 8, 2008, Patrick French asserts that, in spite of instability, terrorist attacks, and other signs of unrest, "India remains the developing world's most successful experiment in free, plural, large-scale political collaboration." French writes of misguided blame placed on India for Islamist fundamentalist attacks on Mumbai that occurred near the time of his article. He writes of the complexity of politics in Pakistan and of fundamentalist hatred that makes no room for nuances and inspires the destruction of a wide range of enemies, in this case including India.

According to another article of the same date, Indian Muslims marched to protest terrorism and to demonstrate their loyalty to India. Since the terrorist attacks of September 11, 2001, many people have made an unfortunate and unfair connection between the Islamic faith and terrorism. The Muslims in India who participated in the protest mentioned above bravely stepped forth to urge people past that narrow view. As this minority group often fights for rights and recognition in India, their actions were especially complicated and difficult. Over the years, both Hindu nationalist groups and Muslims have committed acts of aggression and violence amid the endless religious tension in India.

More recently, the Congress Party seems to be coming back strong. On May 17, 2009, the party surprised the nation—and itself—with a strong victory. It overcame the same regional factions and opposition parties that Indira faced, including the BJP and the Communist Party. The star of the BJP is the controversial Feroze Varun Gandhi, one grandchild who is described as an estranged member of the Nehru-Gandhi family. Another of Indira's grandchildren, Rahul Gandhi, was a favored member of the Congress Party. He earned respect by campaigning tirelessly and hitting an average of four rallies a day. The party's president is Indira's daughter-in-law, Sonia Gandhi. As Indira had hoped, this new unity was expected to facilitate policies to help India's current struggles, predominantly with the economy.

Rahul Gandhi at the 83rd plenary session of India's Congress Party in New Delhi, 2010

CHAPTER SEVEN

Indira Is Herself

INDIRA GANDHI WAS A POWERFUL, PERPLEXING figure. Clearly she felt great pride in and responsibility for her country. The political was always personal for her. She has not always been taken on her own terms, but was often been compared to men, particularly to her father. She is described as being much more pragmatic, and perhaps less idealistic, than Jawaharlal Nehru. In some ways, she was more forceful. She once said that her father was a saint who strayed into politics. Indira continued Nehru's nonalignment policies but was more aggressive as she did so. Her style was more confrontational and less diplomatic than his, but perhaps this was because she came up against the old guard in ways he never had to.

How much did Indira's womanhood define who she was as a leader? It is impossible to say for sure. At an international conference on women in Mexico in 1975, Indira Gandhi described herself as not being a traditional feminist. One of her first and most important influences was her mother, of whom she states,

> She was a convinced feminist, a position which I didn't understand then because I felt that I could do what I liked and that it didn't make any difference whether I was a boy or a girl. In her childhood, my mother had felt the disadvantages of being a girl and being forbidden to do many things which a boy could do.

Indira Gandhi, 1984

Indira said she grew up climbing trees, flying kites, and playing with boys. She criticized Western women for trying to be like men. She said, "To be liberated, a woman should be free to be herself. Rivalry between women and men is unnecessary, in fact it is destructive and itself a bondage."

Indira's work did not appear to focus on women, yet that does not mean women's rights did not matter to her. In 1971, she appointed the Committee on the Status of Women in India, which presented damning conclusions, but she herself made little commentary on it. In her sixth Five Year Plan of 1980 to 1985, she called for the improvement of education, health, and social welfare for women and support for working women, especially those who were self-employed. It is not fair to say that Indira did not care about women. Her main focus, though, was on poverty, a huge issue that dominated Indians' concerns.

Emmanuel Pouchepadass, who introduced and presented Indira's autobiography, *My Truth*, feels that gender did play a role in her leadership, mostly because of how others viewed and treated her. He talks of the charges against her and her son Sanjay for alleged abuses during the state of emergency, and regarding people's passionate objections to Indira's decisions he says, "There is also at the bottom of all this the underhand vengeance of phallocrats ashamed of having allowed themselves to be governed by a woman for such a long time." Certainly people cast gender-oriented critiques and comments her way; for example, some said that she "wore the pants" in the government. Indira's desire to transcend gender could well have been in part a reasonable response toward people who made too much of it—and in negative ways.

Indira and her father accomplished an amazing democratic success in India. Asia today is one of the world's most dynamic places, economically and otherwise, yet many people there do not have political voices. Many countries' leaders claim that democracy is not compatible with their cultural manners and heritage, yet India offers a powerful challenge to this view. Although Nehru and his compatriots looked to the West for models as they built their new democracy, India can also offer instruction for other democracies, with its community and group rights, large-scale multicultural political unions, and triumph despite economic difficulties.

What we say about gender has a lot to do with how we define gender in the first place. Much of the commentary describing Indira Gandhi as being like a man relies on stereotypes, and it probably says more about those offering the analysis than it says of her. She was a strong-willed, intelligent, caring, conflicted, and complex person and national leader. Does it matter that she was female, beyond demonstrating that a woman can achieve anything?

TIMELINE

1917 — Indira is born on November 19 in Allahabad.

1930 — Mahatma Gandhi leads the Salt March.

1931 — Grandfather dies; Indira meets Feroze Gandhi, her future husband.

1934–1935 — Studies with Tagore; studies abroad at Oxford University.

1936 — Mother dies on February 23.

1937 — Travels around Southeast Asia with Jawaharlal Nehru; travels around Europe.

1941 — Returns to India after six years away.

1944 — First son, Rajiv, is born.

1946 — Second son, Sanjay, is born.

1948 — India achieves independence, August 15; Jawarlal Nehru becomes prime minister; Indira meets with Mahatma Gandhi on January 29, one day before his assassination.

1953 — Visits China and meets with Chou En-lai and Mao Tse-tung.

1956 — Becomes president of the Allahabad Congress Party.

1957 — Elected to the Central Election Committee.

1959	Elected president of the Congress Party.
1960	Feroze Gandhi dies.
1962	China attacks India in October; on November 21, a cease-fire is achieved.
1964	Jawaralal Nehru dies on May 27; Shastri becomes prime minister; Indira becomes minister of information and broadcasting.
1966	Shastri dies on January 10; on January 19, Indira is elected leader of the Congress Parliamentary Group; on January 24, Indira is sworn in as India's third prime minister; from March 28 to April 1, Indira makes an official visit to the United States and President Johnson and also meets with President de Gaulle in Paris and Prime Minister Wilson in London.
1967	General elections in India; the Congress Party loses seats, but Indira is unanimously elected leader.
1969	The Congress Party splits on August 20; Indira is asked to leave the Indian National Congress on November 12.
1971	Reelected as leader of the Congress Parliamentary Party and prime minister on March 1; war with Pakistan over Bangladesh (Western Pakistan); Bangladesh wins independence from Pakistan.
1975	Proclaims a state of emergency.
1984	Assassinated by a Sikh guard on October 31.
1991	Rajiv Gandhi is assassinated.

SOURCE NOTES

Boxed quotes unless otherwise noted

CHAPTER 1

p. 5, Stanley Wolpert. *A New History of India, Fourth Edition* (New York: Oxford University Press, 1993), p. 396.

p. 6, par. 2, Edward Luce, *In Spite of the Gods: The Strange Rise of Modern India* (New York: Doubleday, 2007), p. 9.

p. 13, par. 1, Ibid., p. 5.

p. 13, Mary G. Carras, "Indira Gandhi: Gender and Foreign Policy." In *Women in World Politics, An Introduction*, Francine D'Amico and Peter R Beckman, eds. (Westport CT: Bergin and Garvey: London, 1995), p. 5.

CHAPTER 2

p. 19, par. 1, Pupul Jayakar, *Indira Gandhi: An Intimate Biography* (New York: Pantheon Books, 1988), p. 40. **(**Note: Pupul Jayakar was a close friend of Indira Gandhi's, and much of her biography is based on personal interviews over the years.)

p. 19, Indira Gandhi, *My Truth*. Presented by Emmanuel Pouchpadass (New York: Grove Press, Inc, 1980), p. 12.

p. 23, par. 2 (long quotation), Ibid., p. 27.

p. 23, par. 3, Jayakar, p. 47.

p. 25, Jawaharlal Nehru, *Glimpses of World History, Fourth Edition* (London: L. Drummond, 1949), pp. 1-3.

p. 27, Gandhi, p. 22.

CHAPTER 3

p. 29, par. 1 (long quotation), Jayakar, p. 98.

p. 32, Gandhi, p. 51.

p. 33, par. 2, Ibid., pp. 51-53.

p. 33, par. 3, (Motherhood), Ibid., p. 54.

p. 34, Ibid., p. 56.

p. 36, Ibid., pp. 64-65. (Note: Gandhiji is a familiar term of endearment used by Indira, her family, and others who were personally close to Gandhi. Mahatma is the formal term for "blessed one," similar to the word "saint.")

p. 37, par. 1 (long quotation), Jayakar, p. 148.

p. 41, Jayakar, pp. 113-122.

p. 41, par. 3, Ibid., p. 125.

CHAPTER 4

p. 43, par. 1, Jayakar, pp. 126-129.

p. 43, par. 2, Lukas, "She Stands Remarkably Alone", in Jayakar, p. 133.

p. 45, par. 3, Jayakar, p. 146.

p. 47, Ibid., p. 310.

p. 48, par. 2, Frank, pp. 321-322.

p. 52, par. 1, Jayakar, quoting Power, pp. 179-189.

p. 52, Frank, p. 347.

p. 53, par. 1, Jayakar, p. 186.

p. 54, par. 1, Ibid, pp. 190-191.

CHAPTER 5

p. 58, Gandhi, Postface, p. 194.

p. 58, par. 4, Frank, p. 385.

p. 59, par. 1, (long quotation) Gandhi, pp. 161-162.

p. 61, par. 2 (long quotation), Henry Christman, ed., Introduction. *Indira Gandhi Speaks on Democracy, Socialism, and Third World Nonalignment* (New York: Taplinger Publishing Co, 1975), p.7.

p. 61, par. 2 (second long quotation), Ibid., p. 14.

p. 62, Gandhi, p. 168.

p. 63, par. 1, Ibid., p. 170.

p. 63, par. 2 (long quotation), Frank, p. 410.

CHAPTER 6

p. 68, par. 4, Jayakar, p. 347.

p. 71, Gandhi, p. 173.

p. 73, par. 1, Frank, pp. 471-472.

p. 73, par. 2, Wolpert, p. 418.

p. 76, Ibid, p. 487 (From Indira Gandhi, *Remembered Moments*), p. 79.

p. 77, Jayakar, p. 373.

CHAPTER 7

p. 81, Gandhi, p. 23.

p. 82, par. 1, Jayakar, p. 200.

p. 82, par. 3, Gandhi, Postface, p. 93.

FURTHER INFORMATION

BOOKS

Breuilly, Elizabeth, Joanne O'Brien, Martin Palmer, Martin E. Marty, ed. *Religions of the World: The Illustrated Guide to Origins, Beliefs, Traditions & Festivals*. New York: Facts on File, 2005.

Mukherjee, Bharati, and Eric Meola. *India: In Word and Image*. New York: Welcome Books, 2008.

O'Brien, Perry Edmond. *After Gandhi: One Hundred Years of Nonviolent Resistance*. Watertown, MA: Charlesbridge Publishing, 2009.

Srinivasan, Radhika, Leslie Jermyn, and Roseline Lum. *India*. (Cultures of the World). New York: Marshall Cavendish Benchmark, 2011.

DVDS

The Dynasty: The Nehru-Gandhi Story. Produced and directed by Mark Anderson and Charles Bruce. WGBH/Boston and Brook Associates in association with the BBC and Canal Plus, PBS Home Video, 1997.

Gandhi. Directed by Richard Attenborough. Starring Ben Kingsley and John Gielgud. PG, 1982

Mr. and Mrs. Iyer. Directed by Aparna Sen. Starring Rahul Bose and Konkona Sen Sharma. 2002.

BIBLIOGRAPHY

Bose, Nemai Sadhan. *Indira Gandhi: On Herself and Her Times. Her Last and Only Autobiographical Interview*. Calcutta: Ananda Publishers Pvt Ltd, 1987.

Carras, Mary G. "Indira Gandhi: Gender and Foreign Policy," *Women in World Politics, An Introduction*, Francine D'Amico and Peter R. Beckman, Ed. Westport, CT: Bergin and Garvey, 1995.

Christman, Henry, editor, Introduction. *Indira Gandhi Speaks on Democracy, Socialism, and Third World Nonalignment*. New York: Taplinger Publishing Co, 1975.

Dommermuth-Costa, Carol. *Indira Gandhi: Daughter of India*. Minneapolis: Lerner Publications Company, 2002.

Frank, Katherine. *Indira: The Life of Indira Nehru Gandhi*. Boston: Houghton Mifflin Co, 2002.

French, Patrick. "They Hate Us—and India Is Us." *New York Times*, December 8, 2008.

Gandhi, Indira, presented by Emmanuel Pouchepadass. *My Truth*. New York: Grove Press, 1980.

Jayakar, Pupul. *Indira Gandhi: An Intimate Biography*. New York: Pantheon Books, 1988.

Khilnani, Sunil. *The Idea of India*. New York: Farrar, Straus, Giroux, 1999.

Luce, Edward. *In Spite of the Gods: The Strange Rise of Modern India.* New York: Doubleday, 2007.

Morgan, Diane. *The Best Guide to Eastern Philosophy and Religion: Whether You're a Believer, a Seeker, or Just Inquisitive, This Guide Is for You.* New York: Renaissance Books, 2001.

Sengupta, Somini. "India's Governing Coalition Scores Decisive Victory in Parliamentary Races." *New York Times*, May 17, 2009, p. 6.

Wolpert, Stanley. *India.* Berkeley: University of California Press, 1991.

Wolpert, Stanley. *A New History of India. Fourth Edition.* New York: Oxford University Press, 1993.

Worth, Robert F. "Muslims in India Put Aside Grievance to Repudiate Terrorism." *New York Times*, December 8, 2008.

INDEX

ABOUT THE AUTHOR

SARA SCHUPACK grew up in Mill Valley, California, where she came to her love of the ocean, books, and imagination. She studied literature and creative writing on the East Coast for her undergraduate and graduate schooling, and then traveled further east, to Hong Kong, where she lived for eleven years teaching English and learning Cantonese. She has taught English in middle school, high school, and college classrooms for over twenty years. Currently she studies in a doctoral program in education in western Massachusetts, where she lives with her son, Teddy, and his parakeet, Jolie. She remains humbled by and grateful to each and every one of her students. Her previous publications include fiction and creative nonfiction in *Digital Paper*, "There is an 'I' in Community" in *College Composition and Communication*, and also for Marshall Cavendish, *Shakespeare Explained: The Merchant of Venice*.